Life's Delicate Balance

Nellie McLaughlin, a native of Inishowen, Co. Donegal, is a member of the Congregation of the Sisters of Mercy, Northern Province, Ireland. A founding member of The Green Sod Land Trust, Ireland, she is particularly interested in the areas of cosmology, ecology and creation spirituality. She is the author of *Out of Wonder: The Evolving Story of the Universe* (Veritas, 2004).

Life's Delicate Balance

OUR COMMON HOME & *LAUDATO SI'*

NELLIE MCLAUGHLIN

VERITAS

Published 2015 by
Veritas Publications
7–8 Lower Abbey Street
Dublin 1, Ireland
publications@veritas.ie
www.veritas.ie

ISBN 978 1 84730 598 5

Lines from 'Poplar Memory' by Patrick Kavanagh, taken from *Patrick Kavanagh: Collected Poems*, edited by Antoinette Quinn (Dublin: Allen Lane, 2004). Reprinted by kind permission of the Trustees of the Estate of the late Katherine B. Kavanagh, through the Jonathan Williams Literary Agency.

'There's a Dream' by Carmel Bracken RSM, Northern Provence, Ireland. Used with permission.

10 9 8 7 6 5 4 3 2 1

A catalogue record for this book is available from the British Library.

Designed by Heather Costello, Veritas Publications
Printed by eprint Ltd, Dublin

Veritas books are printed on paper made from the wood pulp of managed forests. For every tree felled, at least one tree is planted, thereby renewing natural resources.

Contents

Introduction

Pope Francis' landmark encyclical *Laudato Si'* was launched in Rome on 18 June 2015. This publication, subtitled *On Care For Our Common Home*, is unprecedented in focusing on the subject of the environment. While previous popes, notably St John XXIII, Blessed Pope Paul VI, St John Paul II and Pope Benedict XVI, all spoke on the environment, this is the first time that an entire encyclical has been devoted to the environment and human ecology.

This is Pope Francis' second encyclical, following *Lumen Fidei*, and the timing couldn't be more appropriate. The year began with the United Nations declaring 2015 the International Year of Light and Light-based Technologies and of Soils. Pope Francis chose Pentecost as the issue date for his latest encyclical, the spirit of enlightenment: 'I still have many things to say to you, but you cannot bear them now. When the Spirit of truth comes, he will guide you into all the truth' (Jn 16:12-13).

In highlighting the International Year of Soils, the UN is seeking to draw our attention to how precious and vital soil is for life. 'The soil is a magic place where the alchemy takes place that enables living forms to survive.'[1] It plays a crucial role in climate regulation as our second largest store of carbon after the oceans. The alarming deterioration and loss of this living resource has huge implications for biodiversity, sustainable agriculture, food security and world poverty; it also has a particularly detrimental impact on the economically disadvantaged in our world, a theme central to *Laudato Si'*.

For the United Nations, 2015 is a pivotal year with no fewer than three major summits seeking potentially transformative agreements for radical change, for both people living in extreme poverty and for the impoverished earth. *Laudato Si'* comes midway through the year, just before the first of the major summits. In July, the first of these summits was held in Addis Ababa, Ethiopia, on the crucial issue of financing for development. In September, Pope Francis will address the UN General Assembly in New York, when world leaders will be challenged to sign up to the new Sustainable Development Goals 2015–2030, successor to the Millennium Development Goals 2000–2015. Then, finally, world leaders will gather in Paris in December to endeavour to agree a deal on tackling climate change by setting limits on carbon emissions and terms of accountability.

The UN Conference of Parties started in 1992. This will be the twenty-first such meeting of world leaders since then, hence the conference title, COP 21. Pope Francis recalls the 1992 Earth Summit in Rio de Janeiro, which proclaimed that 'human beings are at the centre of concerns for sustainable development'[2] (167). Many will remember this summit for setting the goal of limiting greenhouse gas emissions in an effort to reverse the trend of global warming worldwide. More than twenty years later one wonders what, if anything, has been achieved?

In his introduction to *Laudato Si'*, Pope Francis reminds us of his patron and inspiration, St Francis of Assisi, who 'was particularly concerned for God's creation and for the poor and outcast' (10). He accredits St Francis with what, to my mind, sums up this much anticipated encyclical: 'He shows us just how inseparable the bond is between concern for nature, justice for the poor, commitment to society, and inner peace' (10).

He expresses the hope that this encyclical letter – now added to the compendium of Catholic Social Teaching – can help us to acknowledge and respond to the 'urgency of the challenge we face' (15). Catholic Social Teaching began formally in 1891 when Pope Leo XIII wrote his encyclical, *Rerum Novarum: On the Condition of Labour*, a response to industrial capitalism. The body of Catholic Social Teaching was further advanced in particular by St John XXIII's *Pacem in Terris* as the world teetered 'on the brink of nuclear crisis' (3) and the documents of Vatican II, notably *Gaudium et Spes:*

Pastoral Constitution on the Church in the Modern World, published in 1965. *Laudato Si'* ushers in a new phase by embracing all of creation directly.

Laudato Si' is a wide-ranging, comprehensive and positively disturbing call to our deepest selves to awaken and act in unison for the common good. Time is running out for our planet and for the impoverished millions in the community of all life. However, this encyclical is not simply an issue-based document; it goes to the heart of the matter, challenging our perceptions, values and behaviours. It is a heart-to-heart conversation, direct, convincing, encouraging, compassionate and compelling – one is almost 'shamed' into action. Significantly, Pope Francis states very clearly that 'the Church does not presume to settle scientific questions or to replace politics' (188), rather it is interested in honest and open debate.

I will review this clarion call under three main headings:
‣ The invitation to come home to our true selves and our rightful place in the web of life;
‣ Widening our circle of compassion to embrace all beings;
‣ The urgent appeal for concerted action on behalf of the most vulnerable.

I also include some core questions for reflection and action. As we enter into the spirit and urgent message of this timely encyclical, may we be emboldened in our hearts and actions.

We shape clay into a pot, but it is the emptiness inside that holds whatever we want.[3]

Endnotes

1. Brian Swimme and Thomas Berry, *The Universe Story* (San Francisco: HarperSanFrancisco, 1992), p. 244.
2. *Rio Declaration on Environment and Development* (14 June 1992), Principle 1.
3. Lao Tzu (571–31 BC), Chinese philosopher and poet.

Come Home:
THE INVITATION

Like his predecessor, St John XXIII, who addressed his letter *Pacem in Terris*, to 'all men and women of good will', Pope Francis states: 'I wish to address every person living on this planet … I would like to enter into dialogue with all people about our common home' (3). In my response to *Laudato Si'* I feel privileged to take up that invitation to enter into dialogue with what is indeed an insightful and critical contribution at this time.

> *I urgently appeal, then, for a new dialogue about how we are shaping the future of our planet. We need a conversation which includes everyone, since the environmental challenge we are undergoing, and its human roots, concern and affect us all.* (14)

The choice of the phrase 'our common home' in the subtitle is radical in that it highlights our shared space as the entire community of life. The Greek word *oikos* – meaning home or household – has the same root for ecology, ecumenism and economy, three major themes throughout the encyclical. There is a golden thread running through the document, a mantra-like refrain reminding us that 'all is connected', each with intrinsic value (33), each a distinct manifestation of the divine (69) and each one dependent on the other: 'Because all creatures are connected, each must be cherished with love and respect, for all of us as living creatures are dependent on one another' (42).

The call to come home, to who we really are as one species among all other species in the wondrous web of life, is set in the ethical framework of harmonious relations central to the Judeo-Christian faith tradition. This harmony is characteristic of all monotheistic faith traditions. It consists of multiple relationships: with self, God, other people and creation in its entirety.

> *Disregard for the duty to cultivate and maintain a proper relationship with my neighbour, for whose care and custody I am responsible, ruins my relationship with my own self, with others, with God and with the earth.* (70)

Harmony in Right Relations

It is true to say that ethically the relationship with self, God and other people has traditionally been to the fore, while our relationship with creation has not been regarded as a moral issue. This is beginning to change with the emerging understanding that all is one, each being unique but not separate in the awesome web of life. 'The universe as a whole, in all its manifold relationships, shows forth the inexhaustible riches of God' (86).

This echoes the profound wisdom of St Thomas Aquinas, who understood that God's goodness 'could not be fittingly represented by any one creature', hence the need to create an array of creatures so that what was wanting in one might be supplied by another in representing the divine goodness.[1] This truth is poignantly described by Passionist priest and cosmologist, Thomas Berry: 'We should be clear about what happens when we destroy the living forms of the planet. The first consequence is that we destroy modes of divine presence. If we have a wonderful sense of the divine, it is because we live amid such awesome magnificence.'[2] The unity and oneness at the heart of creation is central to the teaching of Jesus; indeed it was for this that he gave his life – that all may be one (Jn 17:11).

The journey to reconnect with our deepest roots in the web of life (216) presupposes, I believe, the acknowledgement of our most profound selves, our essence. 'The only journey is the one within.'[3] Pope Francis draws attention to this truth time and again: 'We are able to take an honest look at ourselves' (205) ... 'postmodern humanity has not yet achieved a new self-awareness capable of offering guidance and direction, and this lack of identity is a source of anxiety' (203). He relates inner peace to care for the earth and the common good, noting that it is reflected in a balanced lifestyle and 'a capacity for wonder which takes us to a deeper understanding of life' (225). We are God's work of art (cf. Eph 2:10), born with pure essence:

> I am the fiery life of the essence of God:
> I flame above the beauty of the fields;
> I shine in the waters;
> I burn in the sun, the moon, and the stars
> And, with the airy wind, I quicken all things vitally
> by
> an unseen all-sustaining life ...[4]

We are gifted with divine qualities like love, generosity, beauty, gratitude and compassion. However, as we engage the relationships and complexities of life we develop an ego self for protection, which can stifle the essential self if we allow it to become compulsive. This journey from ego back to essence is the stuff of living, which Pope Francis identifies in *Laudato Si'*, especially in what is happening to the human spirit and to our common home. The challenge of balance is ever before us: 'Most of us are moving through such an undergrowth of excess that we cannot sense the shape of ourselves anymore.'[5]

We are summoned to an ecological conversion (216–221), which is both a conversion of heart and a community conversion. A commitment of this magnitude 'cannot be sustained by doctrine alone, without a spirituality capable of inspiring us, without an "interior impulse which encourages, motivates, nourishes and gives meaning to our individual and communal activity'"(216).[6]

Pope Francis poses the question about what kind of world we want to leave to those who come after us as a way into the deeper concerns and questions we must ponder in our hearts: 'What is the purpose of our life in this world? Why are we here? What is the goal of our work and all our efforts? What need does the earth have of us?' (160). As we ponder these and related questions in our deepest selves may we become a more compassionate presence in our world, being more attuned to the cry of the earth and the most vulnerable among us.

> Love all of God's creation, the whole and every grain of sand in it. Love every leaf, every ray of God's light. Love the animals, love the plants, love everything. If you love everything, you will perceive the divine mystery in things.[7]

Cultivating the harmony in right relationships is crucial as we face the unprecedented challenges of today. There is still evidence of early Greek influence in the dualisms we perpetuate: for example, sacred versus secular; religion versus science; spirit versus matter; and of mechanistic thinking from Newtonian physics in viewing our world as a great machine rather than as a living system. This has profound implications for us spiritually, socially and environmentally. So much is ruptured because of the separations we create and set in stone, and the divisions that cripple us from being our best selves: '… unity is greater than conflict' (198).[8] It is time to commit to what unites us, 'to live in communion with God, with others and with all creatures' (240). We belong together; we are one. May the beauty within us, our innate dignity and interiority, which we share with all beings, open our eyes, hearts and arms to what Thomas Merton calls 'the secret beauty' behind the eyes of every being.

Our Deepest Roots

As we reconnect with our deepest roots in the web of life and remain true to our essence, new horizons open up to counter the devastation of our individually and collectively ego-propelled madness. 'There can be no renewal of our relationship with nature without a renewal of humanity itself' (118). The inner and outer are one and the same journey. 'I express myself in expressing the world; in my effort to decipher the sacredness of the world, I explore my own' (85).[9] We are slowly realising that we can't change what's going on *around* us until we start changing what's going on *within* us:

> Our outer environment can only begin to be healed by our inner, and I'm not sure we can ever truly tend to our polluted waters, our shrinking forests, the madness we've loosed on the air until we begin to

try to clean up the inner waters, and attend to the embattled wild spaces within us.[10]

Meister Eckhart reminds us that, 'The outer work can never be great if the inner work is small, and the outer work can never be small if the inner work is great.'

Entering authentically and critically into what is happening to our common home and humbly acknowledging our human implication in today's ecological crisis can only be possible by consciously entering our heart space, by coming home in a primal sense. In the sanctity of our deepest selves we are nudged to be awake and attentive to our intrinsic wholesomeness and to the beauty and complexity of life as it unfolds. When I'm in touch with and appreciate my own interiority I will be more open to the interiority of all. Mindfulness meditation practice and 'Centering Prayer' help us to stay focused and connected in a fundamental way. Pope Francis introduces the term 'rapidification' (18) – an intensified pace of life and change affecting humanity and the planet. One thinks of phrases such as 'rat-race', 'riding rough-shod over' 'disposable', 'dispensable' and 'throw-away'. This contrasts with the naturally slow pace of biological evolution.

I'm reminded of the story of the caterpillar becoming a butterfly and how time is of the essence in the emergence of new life. The story tells of a man who, witnessing the chrysalis struggle and wanting to assist, inadvertently caused death by hurrying the process. Undoubtedly many of us can recall similar instances of impatience or times when 'we know better' in our own lives. The attitude and practice of going inward, taking time to reflect and being at one with everything speaks of fallow time (237), of jubilee year and Sabbath rest in Judeo-Christian wisdom. 'No-one can cultivate a sober and satisfying life without being at peace with him or herself' (225) ... 'we are speaking of an attitude of the heart, one which approaches life with serene attentiveness' (226).

The invitation to come home to our true selves challenges us to honour and embrace difference rather than regard it as a threat. We share this planet with countless other species. The ecumenically inclusive nature of Pope Francis' engagement is evident from the start, when he writes 'outside the Catholic Church, other Churches and Christian communities – and other religions as well – have expressed deep concern and offered valuable reflections on issues which all of us find disturbing' (7). He also writes of the importance of showing 'special care for indigenous communities and their cultural traditions' (146), those who are united by the same concern and espouse the wellbeing of the whole.

Pope Francis mentions in particular Patriarch Bartholomew (8), who calls for repentance for the ways in which we have harmed the environment. He points out 'the ethical and spiritual roots of environmental problems' (9) highlighted by

Bartholomew, which require solutions not only in technology but in humanity. These include replacing 'consumption with sacrifice, greed with generosity, wastefulness with a spirit of sharing, an asceticism which "entails learning to give, and not simply to give up. It is a way of loving, of moving gradually away from what I want to what God's world needs. It is liberation from fear, greed and compulsion"[11]'(9). Pope Francis returns to these themes many times as he endeavours to understand the systemic nature of what is happening to our common home.

Laudato Si' – in content, style and spirituality – reflects Pope Francis' lived experience. Growing up in Argentina, living and ministering to the world's poorest has both formed and motivated him to be an uncompromising advocate for the most vulnerable, including the unborn. 'When we fail to acknowledge as part of reality the worth of a poor person, a human embryo, a person with disabilities – to offer just a few examples – it becomes difficult to hear the cry of nature itself; everything is connected' (117). In interconnecting planet and people at a radical level he seeks to explore a more systemic way forward and invites all people to do likewise: 'We require a new and universal solidarity' (14).

In structure, the encyclical can be viewed within the social, liberationist frame of See-Judge-Act. How we see and what we see is crucial to our judging and acting, hence my emphasis in this section on seeing and knowing from our essence, our deepest selves. So often we are ego-driven in our shortsighted, exclusivist and compulsive way of living and acting, often unaware of the consequences for planet and people and indeed for ourselves.

> *The only way to gain power in a world that is moving too fast is to learn to slow down. And the only way to spread one's influence wide is to learn how to go deep. The world we want for ourselves and our children will not emerge from electronic speed but rather from a spiritual stillness that takes root in our souls. Then, and only then, will we create a world that reflects the heart instead of shattering it.*[12]

Questions for Reflection:

‣ What will help me to live more from my essence, my essential self?

‣ What must we do to recover our lost sense of being ONE in the sacred community of creation?

‣ What do I need to unlearn or let go of in order to better serve the common good?

Endnotes

1. Thomas Aquinas, *Summa Theologia*, 1, q. 47, art. 1.
2. Thomas Berry, *The Dream of the Earth* (San Francisco: Sierra Club Books, 1988), p. 11.
3. Rainer Maria Rilke (1875–1926), Bohemian-Austrian poet and novelist.
4. Hildegard of Bingen (1098–1179), Medieval mystic.
5. John O'Donohue in conversation with John Quinn, *Walking on the Pastures of Wonder* (Dublin: Veritas, 2015), p. 115.

6. Pope Francis, Apostolic Exhortation *Evangelii Gaudium* (2013), 261.
7. Fyodor Dostoyevsky, *The Brothers Karamazov* (published as a serial in *The Russian Messenger*, 1880).
8. *Evangelii Gaudium*, 228.
9. Paul Ricoeur, *Philosophie de la Volonté, t. II: Finitude et Culpabilité* (Paris, 2009), 216.
10. Pico Iyer (1957–), British-Indian author.
11. Patriarch Bartholomew, Lecture at the Monastery of Utstein, Norway (23 June 2013).
12. Marianne Williamson, *The Gift of Change: Spiritual Guidance for Living Your Best Life* (New York: Harper Collins, 2004).

Widening Our Circle
of Compassion

'It is only with the heart that one can see rightly. What is essential is invisible to the eyes.'[1]

Let us listen and try to feel anew the cry of the earth and the sobs of the poor so that we may be inspired to action. We should be inspired by the example of six-year-old Peruvian girl Ruby Arizabal who, while attending an interfaith candlelight procession and prayer vigil on the eve of the 2014 UN climate summit in Lima, simply said, 'I've come here because the planet is sad'.[2] Quoting from his Apostolic Exhortation, *Evangelii Gaudium*, Pope Francis tells us:

> Thanks to our bodies, 'God has joined us so closely to the world around us that we can feel the desertification of the soil almost as a physical ailment, and the extinction of a species as a painful disfigurement'.[3]

The belief that 'realities are greater than ideas' (201) is a central theme in *Laudato Si'*. It is Pope Francis' preferred way of responding to the gravity of the ecological crisis. Thomas Reese SJ, senior analyst for the *National Catholic Reporter*, attributes this to his personal encounters with people in the slums of Buenos Aires. Reese cites the willingness of Pope Francis to seek advice and to trust the experts with regard to pollution (20–21), waste (22), climate change (23–25) and biodiversity (32 ff.) For Pope Francis, facts are real. There is no ambiguity; facts can enable us to change our ideas.[4]

The Earth in Context

It is mind-boggling to think that we live in an evolving and expanding universe some fourteen billion years old. Astonishingly, we can observe a mere 5 per cent of the universe, so-called 'ordinary matter'. The other 95 per cent is made up of approximately 70 per cent dark energy and 25 per cent dark matter, both of which are still being explored but remain largely beyond our understanding. The mystery of this is humbling and exciting, especially when we realise that all beings are a microcosm of this reality, which possesses inexhaustible richness and profound mystical depths. Perhaps this is what Pope Francis was alluding to in his introduction to *Laudato Si'*: 'Rather than a problem to be solved, the world is a joyful mystery to be contemplated with gladness and praise' (12).

The UN International Year of Light and Light-based Technologies 2015 is a global initiative bringing together science, engineering and the arts.

The aim is to raise awareness of space exploration and of how optical technologies promote sustainable development and provide solutions to global challenges in energy, health, agriculture, communications and education. Light is our guide to understanding the universe; it is our only connection with the wider universe beyond our solar system.[5] Our ancestors intuited this, as we know both from the number of extraordinary ancient monuments throughout the world celebrating light and the centrality of light in our cultural and religious traditions.

Since the beginning of lunar exploration in the 1960s – when we were able to see planet earth in its entirety from space for the first time – the astonishing beauty and fragility of our common home has been etched in our consciousness. This sight was life changing for some of the early astronauts, one of whom exclaimed: 'I put up my thumb and it blotted out the planet Earth.'[6] Our tiny planet in the Milky Way is abundant but finite; it is incumbent on all of us to live in harmony with its rhythms, as our early ancestors were able to do.

Over time, as the encyclical shows, we have become estranged from our roots, disconnected from the earth, our home, and we have nowhere else to go. 'We experience ourselves as separate from the rest, a kind of optical illusion of consciousness ... Our task must be to free ourselves from this prison by widening our circle of compassion to embrace all living creatures and the whole of nature.'[7] Pope

Francis cites the Earth Charter 2000, 'which asks us to leave behind a period of self-destruction and make a new start' (207).

Moral Imperative

In reviewing *Laudato Si'* as a whole I can identify a close correlation with the UN Sustainable Development Goals 2015–2030, with the addition of Pope Francis' Judeo-Christian biblical, theological and spiritual perspective. This makes the moral imperative explicit as we endeavour to respond to the cry of the earth and the plight of the poor among us. Similarly, the Irish Bishops' Pastoral Reflection on Climate Change, *The Cry of the Earth*, has this moral underpinning.[8] The UN Goals are shaped by the three pillars of sustainability: environmental, social and economic. They include six essential elements: dignity, planet, people, justice, prosperity and partnership.

These essential elements shine through the encyclical like rays of light refracted through a prism. They are made explicit by Pope Francis' uncompromising stance regarding the cry of the earth and the plight of the poor. He emphasises a spiritual rootedness and ethical dimension; we are faced with a moral obligation. There is no hiding place for any of us – we cannot dispose of the problem, as our throwaway culture might suggest – and there is no missed target in our war-torn planet; the earth and the poor are always the victims.

While the UN Millennium Goals 2000–2015 achieved much in terms of providing universal primary education, halting the spread of HIV and AIDS and tackling extreme poverty in particular, there are gaps and none are more glaring than gender inequality and the suffering of women and children. Current estimates indicate that in excess of 70 per cent of the world's poor are women. This is most evident in Sub-Saharan Africa and parts of Asia and South America. While the new Sustainable Development Goals are not yet approved they are more expansive in terms of environmental factors such as food security; sustainable agriculture; clean water and sanitation; sustainable use of marine resources; forests; halting biodiversity loss; and combating climate change.

The new Sustainable Development Goals also include sustainable economic growth, employment and sustainable industrialisation. This is in addition to continuing the fight against poverty, hunger, gender inequality and the promotion of inclusive education, world peace and revitalising global partnerships. The onus will be on world leaders at the UN summit in New York in September, who will be addressed by Pope Francis among others, to agree and sign off on these goals for the future wellbeing of planet and people. 'We cannot have well humans on a sick planet.'[9]

The Web of Life

In his analysis of what is happening to our common home, our magnificent web of life gifted by God, Pope Francis is admirably forthright: 'we were not meant to be inundated by cement, asphalt, glass and metal, and deprived of physical contact with nature' (44). I'm reminded of the beautiful image of Indra's net from the Hindu tradition in which the universe is seen as a great net or web with jewels at each intersection. Each jewel is unique and glistens in the sun. When one looks closely at any one jewel, all the others are reflected in it and it in all the others.

All living beings are jewels in the great net of the universe so when we look reverently at one jewel we see all others reflected therein, and it in all the others. What a wonderful image of the body of Christ or the communion of saints in the Christian tradition. This image is very resonant for me as I read *Laudato Si'* which stresses again and again our dignity, interconnectedness and interdependence as the entire community of creation. 'Everything is interconnected, and this invites us to develop a spirituality of that global solidarity which flows from the mystery of the Trinity' (240).

Let us hold this jewelled metaphor in our hearts as we try to understand what is happening to our common home. May it lead us to that conversion of heart and ever-widening compassion so urgently needed in our moment in history: 'If light is in your heart you will find your way home.'[10] This will mean going beyond local, national and international interests when the common good of our planet requires it. That time is now; earth is pleading with us as never before in the history of humanity.

Pollution and Waste

Pope Francis criticises the various forms of pollution and waste stifling our planet, especially over the past two hundred years, causing serious health problems, particularly among the poor (53). He states that our plundered earth is 'among the most abandoned and maltreated of our poor'; she groans in travail (Rm 8:22). 'We have forgotten that we ourselves are dust of the earth (cf. Gn 2:7); our very bodies are made up of her elements, we breathe her air and receive life and refreshment from her waters' (2). The millions of tons of waste generated by us each year domestically and industrially, most non-biodegradable, some highly toxic and radioactive, are desecrating our picturesque landscape:

> The earth, our home, is beginning to look more and more like an immense pile of filth. In many parts of the planet, the elderly lament that once beautiful landscapes are now covered with rubbish. (21)

This reminds me of Rachel Carson, author of *Silent Spring*, who, in the early 1950s, confronted corporate America with the toxic nature of the pesticide DDT in the water system. She emphasised the truth that if one puts dangerous chemicals into water somewhere, they are putting them into water everywhere because of the systemic nature of our living, breathing planet earth. Putting pesticides in water, air or soil is tantamount to putting them into our own bodies and those of all beings through the water system and food chain.

Pope Francis calls us to account, especially with our advanced technologies; our throwaway culture opposes the wisdom of ecosystems and their natural way of absorbing, reusing and recycling everything. Our industrial prowess has 'not yet managed to adopt a circular model of production, capable of preserving resources for present and future generations' (22).

In addition to pollution and waste, he highlights the issues of water, loss of biodiversity and climate change, stressing the human implication and the adverse effects especially on the poor and most vulnerable worldwide. To add to the pain and injustice, these people are the least responsible, if at all, for the devastation. Pope Francis speaks of the threat to human dignity and the breakdown of society resulting from environmental deterioration, stressing in particular the adverse effect of 'current models of development and our throwaway culture' (43). He is uncompromising with regard to global inequality: '... we cannot adequately combat environmental degradation unless we attend to causes related to human and social degradation' (48).

Debt

Throughout the encyclical, Pope Francis draws particular attention to the debt issue. While access to safe drinking water is a basic and universal right 'our world has a grave social debt towards the poor who lack access to drinking water, because they are denied the right to a life consistent with their inalienable dignity' (30). This social debt can be paid in part by providing funding for the provision of clean water – the poor 'cannot buy bottled water' (48) – and sanitary services.

In his analysis of global inequality he brings 'ecological debt' (51) to the fore by tackling the commercial imbalances between the so-called global north and south. The plundering of natural resources from less economically developed countries, especially by multinational companies, leaves behind a depleted natural environment and devastated local population. Added to the social and ecological debt is the crippling burden of foreign debt (52). Pope Francis clearly challenges the global north and urges that we help pay this debt rather than using it as a control mechanism by 'significantly limiting their consumption of non-renewable energy and by assisting poorer countries to support policies and programmes of sustainable development' (52).

The notion of debt is both fascinating and deeply troubling, particularly when one asks the question: 'who is indebted to whom?' If we look at it from a human-centred, market economic point of view it seems straightforward – money has been borrowed and therefore must be paid back with accrued interest. However, if we view this in its rightful context of the total community of creation then my question becomes: 'who is the real debtor?' Planet earth in its rich abundance and finiteness was here long, long before us; the earth cares for us and all beings. It is home for all, not only for the few who wantonly exploit its richness for their own self-interest, showing a complete disregard for those in need.

Indigenous Knowledge

Indigenous wisdom asks: 'can anyone buy and sell their mother?' One of the more callous practices in our common home today is the trafficking of humans and other beings for profit. As we gaze in horror at the treatment of migrants in the Mediterranean Sea and Indian Ocean should we be surprised? Ancient wisdom cautions: 'what we do the earth we do to ourselves.' We are reminded of this in *Laudato Si'* when Pope Francis, citing biblical wisdom, underlines God's gift to all: 'The earth is the Lord's and all that is in it (Ps 24:1)' and further … 'the Bible has no place for a tyrannical anthropocentricism unconcerned for other creatures' (68).

He further draws on local knowledge by quoting from a pastoral letter from the Portuguese Bishops: 'The environment is part of a logic of receptivity. It is on loan to each generation, which must then hand it on to the next'[11] (159). The ego-driven madness of our current market economy, blinded to the finiteness of resources, must be called to account before our planet burns up or sinks into the ocean depths. The following advertisement is sadly not a one-off: 'To attract companies like yours ... we have felled mountains, razed jungles, filled swamps, moved rivers, relocated towns ... all to make it easier for you and your business to do business here.'[12]

Biodiversity

In continuing his assessment of our common home, Pope Francis rightly stresses the serious loss of biodiversity and focuses on the Amazon and Congo basins, the 'richly biodiverse lungs of our planet' (38) and the plundering role of many transnational corporations. He includes the great aquifers, glaciers, wetlands and coral reefs as he quotes, regarding the latter, from the Catholic Bishops of the Philippines, thereby acknowledging local concerns: 'Who turned the wonderworld of the seas into underwater cemeteries bereft of colour and life?'[13] (41)

Rainforests are widely regarded as our greatest biological treasure. It is estimated that over half of the world's species of (ten million plus) plants, animals and insects live in tropical rainforests. They are also unique stores of carbon, yet we are losing the equivalent of 1.5 acres of rainforest every second. One-fifth of the earth's fresh water is in the Amazon Basin. This is astonishing given that a little over 2 per cent of the earth's abundant water supply is fresh and some two-thirds of this is locked in glaciers and ice caps. While our planet is a liquid planet, most of the water is saltwater and therefore unfit for human or agricultural consumption. This puts into perspective Pope Francis' insistence that all, especially the poor, have access to drinking water (27–31).

The principle of diversity is everywhere evident in our evolving universe, that divine creativity flaring forth in abundance of life, beauty and complexity ... 'everything is, as it were, a caress of God' (84). How often do we stop in wonder and awe at the incredible diversity among peoples and all species, each one unique but not separate in the mystery of creation? 'The Universe is a communion of subjects rather than a collection of objects.'[14] The biodiversity found in our teeming oceans, across the continents, under the soil and in the skies is so crucial to life, prosperity and happiness for all beings. Each has a specific role to play as evident in the great ecosystems of our planet and must be respected in its own right. Pope Francis laments the damage being caused to ecosystems prompting species extinction: 'The great majority become extinct for reasons related to human activity' (33).

Biodiversity plays an essential role in making and maintaining the habitability of the earth for all species. Furthermore, it informs our cultural diversity and is the medium through which we express our aesthetic, spiritual and cultural values:

My father dreamt forests, he is dead –
And there are poplar forests in the waste-places
And on the banks of drains.

When I look up
I see my father
Peering through the branched sky.[15]

We depend on the biodiversity of the planet for our food, fibre, fuel, medicine, shelter, leisure and companionship. We tend to take our rich biodiversity for granted, but constant reminders of vital ecological services are everywhere. There is the constant purification of air and water, decomposition and regeneration of soil fertility, protection from ultra-violet rays, pollination of crops, control of agricultural pests, moderation of temperatures and control of floods and droughts. We now know that if bees were to become extinct – and they are under threat – that we would probably survive for no more than four years after their disappearance.[16]

Awaken our praise and thankfulness
for every being that you have made.
Give us the grace to feel profoundly joined
to everything that is.[17]

Activism

While we should be horrified by this devastation

we should also admire the work of concerned activists like Dorothy Stang, Chico Mendes and Edwin Chota – countless indigenous people and others who gave their lives to save the forests and livelihoods of local people, nations bereft by transnational corporations and vested interests in the so-called global north–south divide. With the widespread destruction of native forests, oceans and land the cry of the earth turns to a moan and the poor become more paralysed, especially women who carry the heaviest burden in trying to provide for their families.

We cannot fail to praise the commitment of international agencies and civil society organisations which draw public attention to these issues and offer critical cooperation, employing legitimate means of pressure, to ensure that each government carries out its proper and inalienable responsibility to preserve its country's environment and natural resources, without capitulating to spurious local or international interests. (38)

Climate Change

Pope Francis is categorical in backing the scientific evidence of climate change and global warming, as well as noting the human implication. The threat posed by climate change has devastating consequences for the planet and impacts most severely on the poorest in our world, those who are least responsible for causing it. One has only to think of the droughts, floods, severe weather changes and subsequent loss of homes, food security, livelihoods and increasing death toll. 'The climate is a common good, belonging to all and meant for all' (23).

The UN Intergovernmental Panel on Climate Change (IPCC) issued its Fifth Assessment Report in 2014 – a stark reminder that our planet is warming and that time is running out regarding emissions limits. UN climate chief, Christiana Figueres, in calling for emissions cuts along with activism at every level: 'Early co-ordinated action among governments at international, national, local and city level, businesses, communities and households everywhere is essential to achieve the best sustainable results.'[18]

Climate change is now widely regarded as the single biggest environmental and humanitarian crisis of our time. The challenge of staying below a two degree (Celsius) rise in temperature would mean, according to Chairman of the IPCC Rajendra Pachauri, a drop by 40 to 70 per cent globally between 2010 and 2050, and falling to zero by 2100.[19] While the rise is due in some way to natural fluctuations over the millennia, the collective scientific evidence is unambiguously pointing to the interference of human beings, especially in the global north.

Climate change is seriously affecting the living systems of our planet. The evidence of rapid and relentless change is very compelling: global temperature rise, shrinking ice sheets, glacial retreat, declining Arctic sea ice, sea-level rise, warming oceans, ocean acidification and extreme weather events worldwide. These changes, mainly due to human intervention, are having a devastating effect on countless species in the oceans, on land and in the skies, as they are uprooted from their natural habitat and unable to adapt to new environments.

It is the poorest who suffer most especially from deforestation, sea-level rise, temperature rise and extreme weather events. They all have life-changing effects resulting in mass migrations, widespread disease and alarming loss of life. The number of environmental refugees is steadily increasing. In the mid-1990s the UN estimated that environmental refugees totalled twenty-five million – greater than all other forms of refugees, social and economic, put together. An added dilemma for environmental refugees is the fact that they do not have any rights. 'They are not recognised by international conventions as refugees; they bear the loss of lives they have left behind, without enjoying any legal protection whatsoever' (25). This is a grave injustice that calls for immediate redress.

The Effects on Irish Farming

Mary Robinson, UN Secretary General's Special Envoy on Climate Change, fears for future generations and calls for urgent action: 'The

Taoiseach and other heads of state have to be saying "We are changing course. We are not going to be doing business as usual".[20] Ireland is still an agricultural country, with this sector producing the most carbon emissions, yet our Climate Bill is so far without a target. Professor John Sweeney, climatologist at NUI, Maynooth, asks: 'How does a 50 per cent increase in dairy output, with no assessment of emissions increases associated with it, square up?'[21]

Ireland has a rich heritage in farming, closeness to the land and appreciation of the earth's bountifulness. It is true to say that since the early settlers we have evolved soul roots in the soil, giving us identity and a deep sense of belonging. However, this is changing rapidly as treasured small family farms are now in transition, with farmers finding it increasingly difficult to survive in a profit-driven, highly industrialised market economy. It is crucial that the heart wisdom of our farmers is not ignored but heeded as we seek ways of caring for our common home. The Irish climate – temperate, abundant rainfall and fertile soils – is conducive to wholesome and diversified agriculture. However, with the effects of climate change the Irish farming community is feeling the challenge of periodic excessive precipitation leading to flooding and devastation of land and livestock. This is particularly difficult for small farmers and organic gardeners whose livelihood depends – often solely – on the land.[22]

Irish agriculture is facing a daunting challenge in lowering carbon emissions and maintaining our 'green' image globally, particularly in light of the government-sponsored Food Harvest 2020. Currently beef and milk production accounts for around 60 per cent of agricultural output. There is the added dilemma with regard to water quality in ensuring farming and nutrient management practices are consistent with international obligations. Eamon Ryan, Green Party Leader, writing shortly after the publication of *Laudato Si'*, stated: 'Irish farmers know more than anyone else what is happening with our climate. They will have a vital role to play and everything to gain from adopting an ecological approach to tending our land.'

The Call to Climate Action

The International Panel on Climate Change (IPCC) predicts that environmental refugees could reach one hundred and fifty million by 2050. The areas most affected are Sub-Saharan Africa, India and Asia. The main threats for environmental refugees include deforestation, soil depletion, food scarcity, desertification, water shortages, extreme poverty, population pressure and poor sanitation. I recall the courageous work of the late Wangari Maathai, who founded the Green Movement in Kenya, and countless others who encouraged the planting of trees in response to the cry of the earth and plight of the poor.

The call to climate action is emerging worldwide. This is evident in campaigns that urge people to relinquish fossil fuels; invest in renewable energy; change lifestyle; protect biodiversity; and seek climate justice with regard to poverty stricken nations. They also call for population management in regard to both capacity and distribution; education in equality; and new forms of economics and politics. As a result, a new paradigm for the future is emerging. National groups are networking globally, particularly through social media, with powerful results from the likes of Greenpeace, the Worldwatch Institute, Avaaz, 350.org, the Mary Robinson Foundation, the United Nations, Friends of the Earth and Trócaire, to name but a few. All of these issues call for honest discussion and action.

In general, the political will is still alarmingly absent. However, the recent G7 Summit's stated commitment to abandoning fossil fuels forever (June 2015) and Norway's parliamentary vote to sell its country's huge shares in companies that mine and burn coal (June 2015) are signs of hope. *Laudato Si'* is a tremendous endorsement of these efforts and the countless efforts of individuals and communities worldwide to save our common home and ensure justice for all. The coming few months leading to COP21 in Paris in December 2015 will unite efforts to ensure that our world leaders act decisively to secure the wellbeing and prosperity of earth and its people. There is no time for procrastination.

The centrality of the planet's living systems in ensuring life, energy and prosperity is explored in *Laudato Si'*, as are the threats to their vibrancy and healthy functioning. All beings need pure air, clean water, fertile soil, sunshine and the company of others to live and develop. Current models of development and technology based on the use of 'highly polluting fossil fuels' (165) are often profit driven, controlled by vested interests, sophisticated marketing techniques, and are strongly influenced by party politics that create havoc in our common home. Recent UN estimates reveal that more than two billion people lack access to drinking water and countless go hungry because of soil deterioration from deforestation and toxins. We see the widespread air pollution, notably in China, Japan and other parts of Asia, with people wearing masks as they go about their daily lives, while numerous others suffer from lack of sunshine.

When one thinks of the global financial crash of 2007–2008 and how the major currencies rallied to bolster the banks, one must wonder if some or all of the planet's living systems were to fail, who or what could bolster them? What if we could no longer breathe fresh air, drink clean water, access fertile soil or sunshine? All the money in the world would be powerless to sustain these vital systems. Does this possibility ever cross our minds? We are at a crisis point as never before in the history of humanity and action is urgently needed.

> *'Only when the last tree has died and the last river has been poisoned and the last fish has been caught will we realise that we cannot eat money'.*[23]

Theologian Anne Primavesi, echoing chapter three of the Book of Ecclesiastes and acutely aware of the vulnerability of all life and living systems, offers the following theological reflection:

> *In this time of climate change*
> *To everything there is just one season;*
> *The time is past when atmospheric CO_2 levels do not rise;*
> *For there is no time when our activities do not contribute to a rise in global temperatures.*
> *It is a time to plant trees, not to cut down forests;*
> *A time to walk lightly on the earth, not to drive;*
> *A time to cherish species, not to kill them;*
> *A time to build up life support systems, and not needlessly to consume or waste them.*[24]

Ecological Conversion

Humanity is being jolted and disturbed by the current state of our common home. Above all, I believe we are being summoned to a new humility: 'We are not God, The Earth was here before us and has been given to us' (67). We are urged to embrace an 'ecological conversion', a change of lifestyle, production, consumption and responsible management of abundant yet finite resources. The idea of infinite or unlimited growth, says Pope Francis, 'is based on the lie that there is an infinite supply of the earth's goods, and this leads to the planet being squeezed dry beyond every limit.' (106)

These UN statistics tell it like it is and they are startling:

- There are twenty-four major life systems – fifteen are already beyond sustainable limits;
- 40 per cent of the world's coral reefs damaged or destroyed;
- Half of the earth's original forests are destroyed;
- Half of the worldwide wetlands were destroyed in the twentieth century alone;
- Species are becoming extinct around one thousand times the natural rate.[25]

Over the past fifty years humanity's demand on nature has far exceeded what the earth can replenish. This is evident from our ecological footprint, as we cut trees faster than they mature, harvest more fish stocks than oceans can replenish and emit more carbon than forests or oceans can absorb. The well-known proverb, 'We do not inherit the earth from our ancestors; we borrow it from our children' reminds us that in many parts of our world the way we live severely compromises the ability of future generations to meet their needs.[26] I recall the cautionary words of Thomas Berry in which he reminds us that planet and people will go into the future together or else both disappear: 'The human community and the natural world will go into the future as a single sacred community or we will both perish on the way.'[27]

'The ecological conversion needed to bring about lasting change is also a community conversion' (219). We are called to change our attitude to and relationship with planet earth and each other. 'We are not faced with two separate crises, one environmental and the other social, but rather one complex crisis which is both social and environmental' (139).

Let us wake up before it is too late. It is astonishing that currently less than 20 per cent of the world's richest people control over 80 per cent of the world's resources and create more than 80 per cent of its waste. Our earth has enough food and nurturance for everyone – the problem is the inequitable distribution of resources. Pope Francis emphasises this glaring injustice by referring to a pastoral letter by the New Zealand Bishops in 2006 in which they ask what the commandment 'thou shalt not kill' means 'when 20 per cent of the world's population consumes resources at a rate that robs the poor nations and future generations of what they need to survive'[28] (95). We need a new way of looking at how our world is functioning; the present model is not serving the common good for the entire community of creation. As Albert Einstein said, 'we cannot solve today's problems with the same mindset that created them'.

The Horrors of Warfare

Towards the end of the section about what is happening to our common home, Pope Francis, drawing on the wisdom of his predecessors, especially St John XXIII and St John Paul II, points to the horror of war, biological weapons and nuclear arms (57). Since war and weaponry in all their guises are, to my mind, the greatest curse of mankind, I would have expected a much stronger condemnation by Pope Francis in the context of our common home.

When we really heed the cry of the earth and the pleas of the poor I can think of no single greater cause of terror and suffering than war and militarism. Would there be hungry, poor or displaced people in such proportions in our world today if the money spent on military training and weapons was directed towards life and wellbeing? And then there are the war crimes, including ethnic cleansing, kidnapping, rape, torture and beatings. Would there be the same alarming loss of biodiversity on our planet if the toxins of war and militarism ceased? One shudders to think of the fallout from toxins caused by increasing military training and warfare released into the atmosphere, water, soil and eventually the food chain and to all beings.

What happens to the bombs, bullets, landmines and discarded weapons? What about the effects of Agent Orange or depleted uranium? Where do these go? An out-of-sight, out-of-mind mentality does not serve us well. Is this devastation to the planet ever mentioned in reports from war scenes? Pope Francis cites the Basel Convention on hazardous waste, 'with its system of reporting, standards and controls' (168). Unfortunately, codes of practice have not always been adhered to throughout history; dumping of all kinds of waste into rivers and oceans around the world is a practice that has led to the destruction of sea life and can have lasting effects on the environment, as well as the people who live in it.

We need more scientific minds engaged in, for example, medical research or renewable technologies, instead of militarism, exploring new forms of chemical, biological, bacteriological and, more recently, autonomous weapons. Count to sixty seconds, and three of the world's children will have died as a result of a lack of safe water/sanitation. Count out another sixty seconds, and within these two minutes the world will have spent $3.4 million on its military.[29] Humanity would be shocked to know the military budget of each nation, even in economically poorer nations. This information is, of course, skilfully camouflaged. What if we were to have a military budget inquiry? Can we afford not to as we try to create a more equitable and just future for all beings?

War begets war and so far we seem powerless to slow or alleviate this egomania. Perhaps if society was to rethink the notion of 'hero', expanding it at least to include the unsung heroines and heroes, we might begin to see the futility of perpetuating war, especially for future generations of the entire community of life. I am not minimising the sacrifice of the millions who fought and continue to fight in wars over the centuries, but the fact is that those left behind had to try to survive and fend for their children in the face of starvation and desperation. As Pope Francis reminds us: 'What would induce anyone, at this stage, to hold on to power only to be remembered for their inability to take action when it was urgent and necessary to do so?' (57)

Children's Rights

Laudato Si' makes many touching and emotional references to the poorest among us, enabling us to better understand their plight. Somewhat surprisingly, Pope Francis doesn't specifically highlight children, though he does refer briefly to them and to the elderly under the culture of relativism, which 'leads to the sexual exploitation of children and abandonment of the elderly who no longer serve our interests' (123). There is startling global evidence of children being tortured, raped, kidnapped, trafficked, forced into labour, warfare and violent crimes. Many have no access to education or basic health services, and countless go hungry. There is an urgent need for the rights of the child to be recognised more widely and to be enshrined in the constitutions of all nations.

Overseas Aid

When UN Secretary General Ban Ki-moon visited Ireland in May 2015, he was generous in his praise for Irish overseas aid, and rightly so, but he also urged a similar commitment in the challenge of climate change. The World Bank states that Ireland is the ninth highest per capita polluter in Europe and each Irish person is responsible for the same amount of carbon emissions as almost one hundred people in the world's poorest countries.[30] While it is commendable that our governments, both in the Republic of Ireland and in Northern Ireland, are doing good work in difficult circumstances, I would urge both governments to take their cue from the economy of the earth – to be courageous and implement policies with a sense of vision, creativity, long-term thinking and with a deep-seated respect for sustainability. In so doing they will be better placed to call us all to action on behalf of planet and people in these critical times: 'We won't have a society if we destroy the environment.'[31]

The Value of Work

Ska Keller, German Green Party MEP, dismisses the view that environmental and ecological concerns should take a back seat to the economy of Europe in recovery. She argues that 'we are only going to get out of this crisis if we're putting our economy on a sustainable field, if we invest in those renewables, energy efficiency, if we transform our economy.' It is vitally important that people have work. I also believe that an economy based on the earth economy will provide ample opportunity for sustainable employment and prosperity.

Laudato Si' stresses the value of work in the service of life and development. Pope Francis recalls his predecessor, St John Paul II, who in his 1981 encyclical *Laborem Exercens: On Human Work*, cited the great tradition of monasticism. While originally the monks 'sought the desert, convinced that it was the best place for encountering the presence of God' (126), St Benedict of Nursia advised the combination of prayer and manual labour, hence the famous *dictum ora et labora* (prayer and labour). This was revolutionary at the time in that personal growth and fulfilment 'came to be sought in the interplay of recollection and work' (126). Work is described as 'a necessity, part of the meaning of life on this earth, a path to growth, human development and personal fulfilment' (128). 'Gardening is an active participation in the deepest mysteries of the Universe.'[32]

Speaking on behalf of the poor, Pope Francis is adamant that financial assistance should be 'a provisional solution' (128) and not a substitute for the broader objective of affording people the dignity of work. Sadly, the orientation of our market-driven economy, solely intent on monetary profits, has too often been to create the technology in order to lay off human workers. 'To stop investing in people, in order to gain greater short-term financial gain, is bad business for society' (128). The message of this encyclical is to continue providing employment through 'productive diversity and business creativity' (128). Protection of smallholders in agriculture and business is crucial to ensure economic viability and freedom (129). Business is regarded as 'a noble vocation' (129) and can be a fruitful source of prosperity, especially if motivated by its service to the common good. It is important that workers are treated honestly, paid fairly and that working conditions honour their dignity.

The Cry of the Earth

In 2009, The Irish Catholic Bishops' Conference published *The Cry of The Earth*, a pastoral reflection on climate change, which was updated in 2014. This well-researched, informative and action-oriented document has remained largely closed to the majority of people. How many regular churchgoers can say that they have heard a sermon on climate change or the environment over the past few years? Will Pope Francis' encyclical be the catalyst for change in this regard? Trócaire and Veritas Publications must be commended for the great work they are doing to make these documents readily available throughout Ireland and beyond. The hope is that not only the Catholic community, but all churches, through their schools, parish committees and various existing groups, will be motivated to action on behalf of our common home. Eco-congregation Ireland (ECI) is taking a leading role in this both at home and abroad, by encouraging churches of all denominations to take an eco approach to worship, lifestyle, property and finance management, community outreach and contact with the developing world.[33]

Questions for Reflection:

‣ Do you agree that we need 'an ecological conversion', a conversion of heart, at this time? Why?

‣ How do we develop reverence and compassion for life in all its forms?

‣ What can I/my family/community/neighbourhood do to safeguard our common home?

Endnotes

1. Antoine de Saint-Exupéry, *The Little Prince*, Chapter 21.
2. *National Catholic Reporter* (January 2014).
3. *Evangelii Gaudium*, 215, quoted in *Laudato Si'*, 89.
4. Thomas Reese SJ, *National Catholic Reporter* (30 July 2015).
5. Brian Cox, *The Wonders of the Universe*, BBC television series.
6. Neil Armstrong (1930–2012) on the first moonwalk in 1969.
7. Albert Einstein (1879–1955).
8. *The Cry of the Earth: A Pastoral Reflection on Climate Change*, Irish Bishops' Conference 2009, updated 2014.
9. Brian Swimme and Thomas Berry, *The Universe Story* (San Francisco: HarperSanFrancisco, 1992), p. 257.
10. Quote by Rumi (1207–73), Persian poet.
11. Portuguese Bishops' Conference, Pastoral Letter *Responsabilidade Solidária pelo Bem Comun* (15 September 2003), 20.
12. Reported in *The Ecologist*, 13 September 2002 (advert placed in *Fortune* magazine by the Philippine Government).

13. Catholic Bishops' Conference of the Philippines, Pastoral Letter *What is Happening to Our Beautiful Land?* (29 June 2017).

14. Brian Swimme and Thomas Berry, *The Universe Story* (San Francisco: HarperSanFrancisco, 1992), p. 243.

15. Patrick Kavanagh, 'Poplar Memory', *Patrick Kavanagh: Collected Poems*, Antoinette Quinn, ed. (Dublin: Allen Lane, 2004), p. 23.

16. Paraphrasing a quote by Albert Einstein.

17. 'A Christian Prayer in union with Creation', *Laudato Si'*, p. 122.

18. *The Irish Times*, Tuesday, 1 April 2014.

19. *The Irish Times*, Monday, 3 November 2014.

20. *The Irish Independent*, Saturday, 20 September 2014, pp. 16–17.

21. *The Irish Times*, Friday, 4 April 2014.

22. Eamon Ryan, 'The pope was right to issue stark message on climate change', *The Irish Independent*, Friday, 19 June 2015.

23. Nineteenth-century Cree Indian proverb.

24. Anne Primavesi, *Gaia and Climate Change: A Theology of Gift Events* (New York: Routledge, 2009), pp. 5–6.

25. Taken from the UN Millennium Assessment Report, 2005.

26. WWF Living Planet Report, summary pages 10 and 24.

27. Thomas Berry, 'The Primordial Imperative', *Earth Ethics*, Vol. 3, No. 2, winter 1992.

28. New Zealand Catholic Bishops' Conference, *Statement on Environmental Issues* (1 September 2006).

29. Taken from Norman Myers and Jennifer Kent, eds., *The New Gaia Atlas of Planet Management* (London: Gaia Books, 2005), p. 278.

30. Éamonn Meehan, Executive Director of Trócaire, 'Letters to the Editor', *The Irish Times*, Monday, 29 June 2015.

31. Margaret Mead (1901–1978), American cultural anthropologist.

32. Thomas Berry, 'Activating a New Prosperity for Our Children', *Occasional Papers*, 1989.

33. Taken from ecocongregationireland.com/about.

Inspired to Action

'The greatest step forward in human evolution was made when society began to help the weak and the poor, instead of oppressing and despising them.'[1]

Laudato Si' urges all of us to act together in response to the cry of the earth and the plight of the poor. 'What kind of world do we want to leave to those who come after us?' (160) Having explored the invitation to come home to who we really are in the total community of creation – and glimpsed something of the need to widen our circle of compassion to embrace all beings – may we be inspired to act with commitment and love for the good of all.

'I pray that, according to the riches of his glory, he may grant that you may be strengthened in your inner being with power through his Spirit, and that Christ may dwell in your hearts through faith, as you are being rooted and grounded in love' (Eph 3:16-17).

The Current Economic System
There is no doubt that our present economic system

is failing us. Pope Francis courageously exposes this fact, doing so with a moral authority lacking in so many world leaders today. Professor Nicholas Stern, a climate expert, endorses this view. Stern said that Pope Francis 'has shown great wisdom and leadership … we can and should be choosing paths of economic development and growth that are sustainable and promote well-being and prosperity'.[2] An economy based on infinite growth with finite resources, on short-term gain for the few with no understanding or regard for the economy of earth is ludicrous and devastating for the entire community of life.

'There is no Plan B because there is no Planet B.' These were the stark words of UN Secretary General Ban Ki-moon at the People's Climate March in New York City, in September 2014. Also startling was Lara Marlowe's *Irish Times* report from a recent climate change gathering in Morocco in June 2015. She quoted Nicolas Hulot, Francois Hollande's special envoy for the protection of the planet, who was told by a female participant: 'In Paris, you will decide who will live and who will die.'[3]

A New Story

Humanity must dig deep for the vision and courage to move forward with commitment to the common good, as advocated throughout *Laudato Si'*. We will need to harness all ways of knowing and relating as one community of life if we are to survive and prosper. Above all, I believe we need a shift in consciousness and a new story. We need to move away from the story of earth as an inert planet, made of resources that exist solely for our benefit, to the story of a new relationship with a living, dynamic, nurturing planet and universe – our common home. 'The earth is our common home. We are intimately interconnected to one another and with all the life systems of the planet.'[4]

It is important to be hopeful as we face an uncertain future. The International Panel on Climate Change, while emphasising the gravity of the issues, also tells us that there is still a window of opportunity if we act without delay, consistently and together as a global community. Pope Francis reassures us that all is not lost; we are capable of rising above ourselves and starting anew despite our mental and social conditioning. He says: 'No system can completely suppress our openness to what is good, true and beautiful, or our God-given ability to respond to his grace at work deep in our hearts' (205). The comforting words from the book of Ruth come to mind:

> *Where you go, I will go;*
> *where you lodge, I will lodge;*
> *your people shall be my people,*
> *and your God my God'*
> (Ruth 1:16)

Dependency–Independency–
Interdependency

I wish to explore this section of *Laudato Si'* through the lens of the continuum of dependency–independency–interdependency. This is both linear and cyclical in the passage of time and changing circumstances of our world. I believe this holds some keys to understanding where we have come from and how we might proceed more respectfully and resolutely as one strand in the magnificent web of life. Earth is approximately 4.5 billion years old, formed within the solar system from spin-off from the swirling sun. Gradually life on earth in all its splendour, variety and complexity emerged: early cellular life, algae, fungi, bacteria, microbes and worms, teeming oceans, reptiles, insects, birds, seeds, flowers and vegetation, mammals and primates.

We emerged within this bountiful creativity of God, our world abuzz with song, play, work, companionship and seething with potential. Pope Francis cites the Judeo-Christian tradition in his analysis of the mystery of the universe: ' ... for it has to do with God's loving plan in which each creature has its own value and significance' (76). The gift of creation is illuminated by God's love 'which calls us together into universal communion' (76). In the human the universe becomes self-conscious; this is both a privilege and a responsibility. Our reflective self-consciousness is influenced by our sensory perceptions – how we feel, see and touch the world around us. The compelling message of *Laudato Si'* brings us to our senses, inviting us to a fresh awareness of the colour, fragrance, music, beauty, variety, challenges and complexities of ourselves and our planet, juxtaposed to its current state. Pope Francis remarks: 'An outsider looking at our world would be amazed at such behaviour, which at times appears self-destructive' (55).

Looking Back to Help Move Forward

'Stop acting so small. You are the universe in ecstatic motion'.[5]

As a child growing up in rural Ireland, I loved the outdoors and sport. I was intrigued by the long jump, and used to practise by standing at one marker and jumping to another one until my father, observing my lack of progress, taught me a new way. He explained that in order to advance the distance I was clearing, I had to go back a number of paces from my take-off marker to get a run at it so that I could go much further with the accelerated speed. It was a eureka moment and I still remember that sense of freedom and excitement. That wisdom inherent in taking the longer view has stayed with me through life, especially in times of decision-making.

In order to move forward, it is wise to gather the ancestral wisdom. We truly stand on the shoulders of giants, the great people who have gone before us, as well as the rock-solid wisdom and energy of the entire community of life stretching back almost fourteen billion years. From this vantage point our view of things has a depth and profundity, as well as the far-sightedness so needed today. Let us step back to glimpse anew our ancestral wisdom and ingenuity, especially the sense of togetherness and identity as one community of life, so that we may be enabled to commit more consciously to the common good of all beings. This is not about going back in the sense of regressing or 'a return to the Stone Age' (114), rather it is about emboldening ourselves intuitively to go forward with greater commitment and resolve.

Our earliest ancestors depended on earth and its inhabitants for their basic needs: food, nurturance, shelter and companionship. Over millennia, as the human presence on earth grew and spread, the transition from a hunter-gatherer society to Neolithic village took place – especially close to the great rivers of the known world – with minimal impact on the wider environment. It wasn't until the agricultural revolution some ten thousand years ago that humans began to move slowly away from that intimacy with earth, which is characteristic of a partnership. For centuries the movement apart was very gradual, but the Industrial Revolution of the seventeenth and eighteenth centuries dealt a decisive blow to that partnership.

The power-driven machinery of the Industrial Revolution changed the course of agriculture, transport, manufacturing and communications. We began to act as though independent of the earth and forged our way deeper and deeper into her systems and processes, even trying to change her geography and geological systems – the fundamental laws of creation. Technological advances over the years have created much that is good; the potential is laudable. It must be developed and expanded, but not at the expense of the poor or the planet. *Laudato Si'* cautions 'never have we hurt and mistreated our common home as we have in the last two hundred years' (53).

However, from the beginning there have been communities – indigenous and otherwise – including our early Irish ancestors, who have maintained these faithful bonds with the earth. 'These people, who touch soul chords within the human psyche, hold, I believe, the earth wisdom and guidance that so many of us seek.'[6]

In many parts of our world today, millions of people are wholly dependent on nature's bounty. I recall with wonder and gratitude time spent with the Northern Cheyenne and Crow Native American people of Montana and Wyoming some years ago. I had the privilege of attending some of their sacred ceremonies, which included sharing food, usually outdoors. Before we partook of the delicious food, the host offered a portion back to the earth in thanksgiving for the gift of nourishment we were about to receive. This reminded me of my childhood, where all was gift as we lived so close to the earth and depended so much on her fruitfulness.

Moving Towards Interdependence

Some persist in believing that humanity can live and prosper independently of the earth. However sophisticated our technology may be we are mistaken in this. We simply have to ask ourselves whether it is possible to live without pure air, clean water, fertile soil, the sun or the companionship of all species? What are we doing to these living systems today? In his analysis of the human roots of the ecological crisis, Pope Francis rightly acknowledges technology's power for good, especially in the areas of medicine, engineering, communications, and aspects of sustainable development (102); however, he warns against the dangers of too much power in the hands of too few. Never before has humanity had such power over itself, 'yet nothing ensures that it will be used wisely, particularly when we consider how it is currently being used' (104).

It is time to move towards greater interdependence as planet and people, and to assist one another in realising this for the common good:

> An interdependent world not only makes us more conscious of the negative effects of certain lifestyles and models of production and consumption which affect us all; more importantly, it motivates us to ensure that solutions are proposed from a global perspective, and not simply to defend the interests of a few countries. (164)

We have become disconnected from the earth; we have lost our sense of who we are and the consequences are dire for our planet and for the most vulnerable. 'We lack an awareness of our common origin, of our mutual belonging, and of a future to be shared with everyone' (202). The renewal and reconnection we seek 'entails a loving awareness that we are not disconnected from the rest of creatures, but joined in a splendid universal communion' (220).

Pope Francis strongly criticises extreme individualism, compulsive consumption, unlimited progress, the unregulated market, the enormous inequalities in our midst, the lack of strong leadership and moral courage, together with the devastation of our common home. He is particularly critical of politicians who refuse to face the challenges of today or who pander to the proponents of profits at any cost: 'The myopia of power politics delays the inclusion of a farsighted environmental agenda within the overall agenda of governments' (178). He advocates that 'we must regain the conviction that we need one another, that we have a shared responsibility for others and the world, and that being good and decent are worth it' (229). While the post-industrial period may be regarded as one of the most irresponsible in history, Pope Francis sees reason to hope that humanity at the dawn of the twenty-first century might 'be remembered for having generously shouldered its grave responsibilities' (165).

Sustainability

Laudato Si' calls for a change of direction; to explore other courses of action; to widen the dialogue; and for all parties concerned to be at the table so that realistic policies, strategies, goals, impact assessments and clear terms of accountability can be explored and agreed. Since 'the excluded' form the majority of the planet's population (49), it is imperative that they have a voice in economic and political discussions and that they are involved in local ecosystem management as a way out of poverty. 'Interdependence obliges us to think of one world with a common plan' (164). Vested interests; short-term thinking; profits at any cost; monocultures; compulsive consumerism; rampant use of finite resources; weak and tardy responses by politicians to challenges; and lack of regulation and controls internationally all contribute to the unhealthy state of our common home and the desperation of the poor and vulnerable.

> *That these centuries of 'progress' should now be ending in increasing stress for the human is the final evidence that what humans do to the outer world they do to their own interior world. As the natural world recedes in its diversity and abundance, so the human finds itself impoverished in its economic resources, in its imaginative powers, in its human sensitivities, and in significant aspects of its intellectual intuitions.[7]*

Sustainability respects the carrying capacity of local ecosystems and aims to integrate existing environmental, social and economic needs without compromising the wellbeing of future generations.[8] The market economy divorced from the economy of earth is both absurd and radically unsustainable. Recalling the financial crisis of 2007–8, Pope Francis laments the fact that the 'opportunity to develop a new economy, more attentive to ethical principles, and new ways of regulating speculative financial practices' (189) has been missed. 'The response to the crisis did not include rethinking the outdated criteria which continue to rule the world' (189). He is forthright in posing the question as to whether it is 'realistic to hope that those who are obsessed with maximising profits will stop to reflect on the environmental damage which they will leave behind for future generations?' (190).

The pace of consumption, waste and environmental devastation can only precipitate catastrophes, as we are already experiencing globally, so that 'we may well be leaving to coming generations debris, desolation and filth' (161). There is an urgent need for longer-term thinking and planning and for more concerted action if all are to feel at home in our common home. 'To restore healthy economic and social function, we must create economic institutions that restore money to its proper role as a facilitator of livelihood creation. This means transforming societies driven by the love of money into societies dedicated to the love of life.'[9]

When our politicians assure us that the economy is improving, what precisely do they mean in terms of the community of life? They are obviously working from a mindset that sees people and planet as separate rather than interconnected and interdependent. We are missing the opportunity to gradually build a more sustainable future where all will count and have access to the earth's finite resources.

Perhaps a high-profile decision, like that taken in the Netherlands in June 2015, will be necessary to spur nations to action. A group of concerned citizens took the case against the government on damages to health grounds. The unprecedented ruling – that the country must cut its greenhouse gas emissions by at least 25 per cent by 2020 – is the first of its kind. With this ruling a government has an independent legal obligation to safeguard its own citizens.[10] Will this create a wave of climate litigation around the world now that a government has been told that it cannot hide behind international negotiations?

Laudato Si' courageously outlines the current state of our common home and our responsibilities towards it. This is a timely affirmation for all the efforts of those working both locally and internationally for eco-justice (211–12). Education and awareness are critical in changing hearts and minds and in inspiring people to action. Pope Francis praises the significant work of global environmental groups, of NGOs and cooperatives. He also praises those who ensure a strong sense of local community – where creativity, responsibility regarding resources and waste, a love of the land

and care of the poor is fostered and maintained. He mentions in particular indigenous peoples whose lifestyle is an embodiment of these values (179).

The journey to interdependence will inevitably mean unlearning much of what many of us have imbibed from the market- and profit-driven economy. This is based on treating resources as though they are infinite; and a belief that humans are separate from and masters of the earth – an object that exists merely for our admiration, benefit, use and abuse. This disconnection must be reconciled so that our major systems – social, economic, political, judicial, religious, education and health – might honour our fundamental interconnectedness. 'Young people demand change. They wonder how anyone can claim to be building a better future without thinking of the environmental crisis and the sufferings of the excluded' (13).

Laudato Si' expands on this by noting that nature is much more than a resource. It points out ways of proceeding, among which are: reclaiming our own dignity and potential for good; consolidating interconnectedness over separation; taking pride in and responsibility for our common home; tuning into the cry of the earth and the plight of the poor among us; and allowing this to change us for the common good. Strategically this will entail: divesting from fossil fuels (165); investing in and developing renewable energy sources; more efficient use of energy; upgrading public transport; planning a sustainable and diversified agriculture;

better management of marine and forest resources and biodiversity protection generally; and ensuring universal access to drinking water (164).

It is also paramount that all people have a voice and a place at the table for planning what they need most, rather than what others perceive they need. This includes more equitable distribution of resources and access to education, health and legal support (183). I firmly believe that the underlying gender inequality must be addressed and resolved as this perpetuates separations that are unjust, alienating and undermining of human dignity. Moreover, it is the same dominant mindset that perpetuates the severance between humanity and planet earth, resulting in continuing exploitation and oppression.

It is heartening to hear of the various efforts for the common good already in operation in our common home. Many of these echo what Pope Francis advocates in *Laudato Si'* and will undoubtedly be affirmed by his support. I wish to cite some of these in the hope that others will be inspired to act. In the words of G. K. Chesterson: 'There is one thing that gives radiance to everything. It is the idea of something around the corner.'

Policies for Change

In trying to develop a more inter-dependent relationship between planet and people and build a mutually sustainable future, the example of Ecuador comes to mind. This nation is the first to include the Rights of Nature in its constitution. This is a great step towards a paradigm shift for humanity. The constitution was re-written in 2007–8 and ratified by the citizens of Ecuador in September 2008. This means that nature is no longer regarded as property under the law; rather it has, in all its forms, the right to exist, maintain and regenerate its vital cycles. In addition, the people have the legal authority to enforce these rights on behalf of the ecosystem and the ecosystem itself can be named as the defendant.

Another inspiring example comes from Costa Rica, a small country in Central America. It is a shining example of how certain economic policies and good governance can turn a country into a relatively sustainable, modern democracy within a few decades. Costa Rica now uses over 99 per cent renewable energy, has managed to keep its Gross National Product (GDP) growing for decades, disbanded its military and directed the funds towards education; it has also transformed itself from one of the most deforested nations to a country with almost 50 per cent forest cover today. As I was reading Pope Francis' 'Lines of Approach and Action' (163–202) section, Costa Rica was foremost in my thoughts.

The journey to greater interdependency of planet and people can take many years. I would like to cite as an example, among a growing number, the work of Trócaire and the courageous steps it is currently taking in this direction. Founded in 1973 by the Catholic Bishops of Ireland in response to the suffering of the world's poorest people, Trócaire came, through its global humanitarian work, to understand the systemic nature of world poverty and oppression. Environmental and social aspects are one and the same, and Trócaire's climate justice campaign highlights this. Extreme poverty, deforestation, soil deterioration, food insecurity, conflict and mass migrations are closely linked to climate change and global warming. The facilitation of diocesan Justice, Peace and Integrity of Creation groups in Ireland by Trócaire is opening up possibilities for people to get involved for the common good of all.

Divesting from Fossil Fuels

The campaign for the divestment of fossil fuels (coal, oil and gas) by grassroots groups is growing ever stronger. The climate group 350.org, with its Fossil Free campaign headed by co-founder Bill McKibben, has gained considerable traction through social media. Greenpeace.org and Avaaz.org are also very proactive when it comes to the plight of the planet and attendant social issues. As indicated earlier, the decision of the recent G7 Summit to commit towards a world free of fossil fuels is a huge boost, with some governments already moving in this direction. Over recent months some churches and religious communities have begun to divest of non-renewable fuels. In the wake of *Laudato Si'*, the Philippines, one of the nations most vulnerable to climate change, has committed to mobilising resources in order to save the planet.[11]

Divesting will be a difficult process given the strong lobby against it. There is the controversial Keystone XL pipeline from Canada to USA and the tar sands drilling in Alberta, as well as the proposed drilling in the Arctic. Nearer home we have the fracking issue, which is expanding in scope in the UK. It is hoped that the moral authority of *Laudato Si'* might act as a reality check for the sake of planet and people. It is encouraging that both USA and China are honouring the landmark agreement they reached in 2014 regarding co-operation on climate change. President Obama unveiled the final shape of his Clean Power Plan in early August 2015, announcing a proposed cut in carbon emissions of 32 per cent by 2030, compared with 2005 levels. This is a brave and timely decision given the strong opposition he will encounter from vested interest groups that profiteer from the excavation of fossil fuels. Likewise, President Xi Jinping has submitted China's intentions to cut its greenhouse emissions per unit of domestic product by 60–65 per cent from 2005 levels to the UN ahead of the Paris meeting in December 2015. Islamic leaders, at their recent symposium in Istanbul in August 2015, urged climate action and pledged to assist fossil fuel divestment.[12]

Naomi Klein, author of *This Changes Everything: Capitalism vs The Climate* and an ardent critic of twenty-first century capitalism, has been invited by Pope Francis to join the Vatican Climate Team. This is a wonderful sign of hope as the Canadian secular Jewish feminist challenges an economic system which puts profit before people and the planet, and that is both fuelling the climate crisis and actively preventing us from taking the necessary actions to avert it. This, she declares, puts climate economics in the realm of ethics and morality.[13] She has said of the fossil fuels industry that it is locking us into a future we can't survive. Even in the midst of greatest pain and desolation, Pope Francis wishes 'to insist that love always proves more powerful' (149). This echoes the intriguing words of Teilhard de Chardin over sixty years ago: 'Someday, after mastering the winds, the waves, the tides and gravity, we shall harness for God the energies of love and then, for a second time in the history of the world, man will have discovered fire.'[14]

Priceless Nature

Pope Francis has made it clear time and again in *Laudato Si'* that the environment, a gift of God, possesses intrinsic value and is more than just a resource (33, 69). 'We can speak of the priority of being over that of *being useful*'[15] (69). It has often been asked in recent times whether we can put a price on nature. We say that it is priceless but in our current economic model it is largely treated as worthless. The economy of earth is not treated as part of our economic system, which was built on the premise of infinite growth on a finite planet.

Because of this the natural environment is seen as something apart from us, at best a resource and is therefore more vulnerable to rampant exploitation. This is true in many parts of our world; the journey to interdependence is an arduous one.

Ireland is already committed, under EU and national legislation, to assess the economic value of our natural capital – air, water, soils, minerals, fossil fuels and all living things – and promote the integration of these values into accounting and reporting systems by 2020. The newly formed Irish Forum on Natural Capital (June 2015) will try to convince people that these resources come at a cost. Dick Ahlstrom, writing in *The Irish Times* recently stated that the forum will seek to inform government, its agencies and the private sector that the services being provided by the planet are not free and that they need support if they are to be sustained.[16] A conservative estimate in 2008 put Ireland's natural capital at €2.6 billion. While it is not possible to quantify nature's bounty in precise terms, the hope is that we will wake up to the pressing need to live more in harmony with the earth's rhythms and dynamic processes rather than blindly assuming we have unlimited access to finite resources.

The Importance of Education

In *Laudato Si'* Pope Francis highlights the crucial role of education in caring for our common home, where planet and people can live in a mutually sustainable fashion (202–215). He identifies the educational challenge of cultivating a generous spirit and ecological sensitivity in the young. A cultural shift is required, as they have grown up in the culture of extreme consumerism and affluence (209).

'Ecological citizenship' (211) is built on sound virtues and on a commitment to do one's best for the sake of the whole. 'Ecological education can take place in a variety of settings: at school, in families, in the media, in catechesis and elsewhere' (213). Political institutions, churches and various social groups have a role to play in raising awareness. The appreciation of beauty is seen as instrumental in our duty of care.

> *If we want to bring about deep change, we need to realise that certain mindsets really do influence our behaviour. Our efforts at education will be inadequate and ineffectual unless we strive to promote a new way of thinking about human beings, life, society and our relationship with nature.* (215)

I would add that the education process must inevitably include learning the story of our evolving and expanding universe and the continuity of life as it shapes us within the larger arc of divine creativity and unfolding. This is critical in understanding our interconnectedness and interdependence as planet and people – a central theme in *Laudato Si'*.

Happiness is one of the aspirations mentioned by Pope Francis. He describes it as follows: 'Happiness means knowing how to limit some needs which only diminish us, and being open to the many different possibilities which life can offer' (223). This connects with his earlier comment arising from an ancient lesson found in many religious traditions, namely, that 'less is more' (222). Perhaps it could be included in our Gross National Product i.e., Gross National Happiness (GNH), as in Bhutan? In 2011 the UN General Assembly passed a resolution making GNH an integral part of the UN's development ideals.[17] In the spirit of *Laudato Si'* as we wake up anew to our own goodness and generosity and our collective responsibility for our common home let us begin to shift our focus from economic growth to growth in wellbeing and happiness for all.

Think Globally, Act Locally

In this encyclical every effort to help the cause, however small or local, is encouraged. This ranges from avoiding the use of plastic and paper, reducing water consumption, separating refuse, cooking only what is needed, to using public transport, car-pooling, planting trees, conserving energy and showing care for all living beings (211). We can take heart from the extent and variety of projects, both environmental and social, throughout Ireland and globally. The following is a national flavour of a larger global tapestry: Green Sod Ireland (land trust), Transition Towns, Be the Change, Eco-congregations, Eco-villages, Community Gardens and Allotments, Bee-keeping, Bird-watching, Seed-Saving, Eco-centres, Justice, Peace and Integrity of Creation Groups, Mercy International Association, Social Justice Ireland, Focus Ireland, Peter Mc Verry Trust, St Vincent de Paul, Simon Community and Barnardos.

In addition, there are the initiatives of many congregations and interest groups together with the thousands, voluntary and otherwise both here and abroad, working with the homeless, migrants, the poor, children at risk, people with special needs, the aged; as well as working for anti-trafficking, debt relief and climate justice. With the Environmental Protection Agency, Ireland, and the Northern Ireland Department of Environment we aspire to bring about a sustainable economy, which is low carbon, resource efficient and climate resilient for the common good. 'Alone we can do so little; together we can do so much.'[18]

Endnotes

1. Maria Montessori (1870–1952), Italian physician and educator.
2. Professor Nicholas Stern, 'Protecting the Environment: The Pope Fills the Leadership Gap Left by the World's Politicians', *The Tablet*, 18 June 2015.
3. *The Irish Times*, Saturday, 6 June 2015.
4. Irish Bishops' Conference, *The Cry of the Earth: A Call to Action for Climate Justice* (2014), p. 18.
5. Rumi, thirteenth-century Persian poet.
6. Nellie McLaughlin, *Out Of Wonder: The Evolving Story of the Universe* (Dublin: Veritas, 2004), p. 169.

7.   Brian Swimme and Thomas Berry, *The Universe Story* (San Francisco: HarperSanFrancisco, 1992), p. 242.
8.   Brundtland Commission Report 'Our Common Future' (1987).
9.   David C. Korten, foreword, in Richard Douthwaite, *The Growth Illusion* (UK: Green Books, 1992, 1999), p. xiii.
10. *The Irish Times*, Business News, Thursday 25 June 2015.
11. Brian Rowe, 'Philippine Church takes lead on Francis' Environment Encyclical', *National Catholic Reporter*, 25 July 2015.
12. Soli Salgado, *National Catholic Reporter*, 19 August 2015.
13. *The Irish Times*, Thursday, 2 July 2015; Ines San Martin, Vatican Correspondent, www.cruxnow.com, 1 July 2015.
14. From 'The Evolution of Chastity', *Toward the Future*, 1936, XI, pp. 86–7.
15. German Bishops' Conference, *Zukunft der Schöpfung – Zukunft der Menschheit. Einklärung der Deutschen Bischofskonferenz zu Fragen der Umwelt und der Energieversorgung*, (1980), II, 2.
16. *The Irish Times*, Monday, 22 June 2015.
17. *Resurgence & Ecologist* magazine, July/August 2015, p. 38.
18. Helen Keller.

Conclusion

Right now, we are at a critical moment in history. Pope Francis says, 'Many things have to change course, but it is we human beings above all who need to change' (202). He adds that 'we can be silent witnesses to terrible injustices if we think we can obtain significant benefits by making the rest of humanity, present and future, pay for the extremely high costs of environmental deterioration' (36). I'm reminded of the challenging words of Confucius: 'To know what is right and not do it is the worst cowardice.' Since 'it cannot be emphasised enough how everything is interconnected' (138), we are urged to think and act strategically in 'an integrated approach to combating poverty, restoring dignity to the excluded, and at the same time protecting nature' (139).

This is also a Kairos moment – a time of opportunity and hope. It is the time when, individually and collectively, we endeavour to take to heart the challenging yet encouraging message of *Laudato Si'* and continue the dialogue, exploring together our oneness in the mystery of the unfolding universe, our common home. This is the time to clarify anew what we cherish most: 'The purpose of our lives is to give birth to the best which is within us.'[1] In the spirit of the Earth Charter (2000) may we summon the belief, courage, vision and commitment to, 'Let ours be a time remembered for the awakening of a new reverence for life, the firm resolve to achieve sustainability, the quickening of the struggle for justice and peace, and the joyful celebration of life'[2] (207).

As we travel 'let us sing as we go' (244), and may the dream never cease to allure us:

There's a dream in my soul that wants to live
A dream of oneness with all that is
A dream of a love that can heal a wounded world
Can you dream this dream with me?

It will take you to places that are torn
Broken apart by war
Places filled with pain and hopes that seem lost
Where colour is but a memory.

Can you trust that you'll never be alone
That there is a pattern to it all
That we are evolving into a better way
And each one has a role they must play.

Can you give of the best of who you are
Unfolding with the mystery of it all

Trusting our earth will soon begin to heal
When all of us awake to who we are.

There's a dream in my soul that wants to live
A dream of oneness with all that is
A dream of a love that can heal a wounded world
Can you dream this dream with me?[3]

Endnotes

1. Marianne Williamson.
2. Earth Charter, The Hague, 29 June 2000.
3. 'There's a Dream' by Carmel Bracken RSM, Northern Province, Ireland.